# VISION BEYOND MEASURE

TULSA

ISBN: 978-1-957262-73-4 (Hardcover)
*Vision Beyond Measure: A 30-day Interactive Devotional to Help You Discover Your Next Step*

Copyright © 2023 by Lewana Harris
All rights reserved.

No part of this publication may be reproduced, distributed, or transmitted in any form or by any means, including photocopying, recording, or other electronic or mechanical methods, without the prior written permission of the publisher, except in the case of brief quotations embodied in critical reviews and certain other noncommercial uses permitted by copyright law.

For permission requests, write to the publisher at the address below.

Yorkshire Publishing
1425 E 41st Pl
Tulsa, OK 74105
www.YorkshirePublishing.com
918.394.2665

Published in the USA

# VISION BEYOND MEASURE

A 30-day Interactive Devotional
to Help You Discover Your Next Step

by
Lewana Harris

This devotional is dedicated to my daughters, Skyler and Madison, and son Bryce. I pray God gives you vision, wisdom, and clarity for everything you are called to accomplish in life. You all are amazing and I love you very much!!!

## Contents

The Power of God's Grace ............................................. 11
We are the Body of Christ ............................................. 14
God Can Still Use You ................................................. 16
Flip the Switch ............................................................ 19
Keep Your Focus on God ............................................. 22
You are Free! ............................................................... 25
Use Your Gift ............................................................... 28
Give God the Glory ..................................................... 31
Be Bold in Your Faith .................................................. 33
Transformational Leadership ....................................... 36
You are Not Forgotten ................................................. 39
Don't Get Weary ......................................................... 42
Now Faith .................................................................... 45
Faith is Action ............................................................. 48
Gifted To Serve ........................................................... 51
The Gift of Discernment ............................................. 52
You are Qualified ........................................................ 54
Blurred Vision ............................................................. 56
God is Still There ........................................................ 59
Be Silent and Trust God ............................................... 62
Take Dominion ........................................................... 65

Renew Your Mind ........................................................... 68
Be All Things ................................................................. 71
Be The Example ............................................................. 74
Heart Posture ................................................................. 77
Just One Word ............................................................... 80
You Can Be Restored ..................................................... 83
Remove the Barrier ........................................................ 86
Speak The Word ............................................................. 89
Forgive ........................................................................... 92

# Foreword

## by Pastor Sandy Scheer, Guts Church

"If you don't quit, you win!" is a statement that unmistakably characterizes the 30-year history of Guts Church, of which Lewana Harris is an Internship graduate. This book is based on her study of the Word during her Internship at Guts Church. Lewana has taken any perceived limit and welcomed the challenge to overcome. She has proudly raised three children on her own, become a leader in her community, and submitted herself to an intense training program in the past year while still working full-time to pursue greater development.

God always has more for us. His desire is for us to walk in purpose and fulfillment. God's Word is the final authority in our lives. Through this devotional, you will find revelation that you were made to be MORE THAN a conqueror and be confident in God's Promise for you.

## The Power of God's Grace

### ACTS 9:15
"But the Lord said to Ananias, "Go! This man is my chosen instrument to proclaim My Name to the Gentiles and their kings and to the people of Israel."

Paul was one of my favorite characters in the Bible because his testimony provides proof that no matter what you have done in your life, God still loves you and is a God of forgiveness.

Paul shares his testimony of how God transformed his life, on the road to Damascus, from persecuting Christians to becoming one of the most committed followers of Christ, professing the Gospel. God chose Saul, changed his name to Paul, and anointed him with the calling of being a witness to all people of what he had seen and heard on that road. He testified in challenging circumstances, even as a prisoner, and this serves as a great testament to his dedication, perseverance, and endurance, knowing that God was with him throughout the entire journey. Paul's experience can encourage you to know and understand that when God has a plan for you, He will meet you right where you are and empower you to influence change in the world to further the Kingdom. I am sure Paul felt guilt, shame, and unworthiness, based on his past experiences. I am

sure he went through a season of feeling inadequate and ill-equipped for the calling on his life. During his time of preaching the Gospel, I am sure there were people who attempted to remind him of his past, as some people do. And I must say, I have felt those same feelings at some point in my life, as well. Feeling that "imposter syndrome." If I had to summarize Paul's life, I would have to point out that at the center of Paul's preaching was God's grace. Additionally, I have learned that if we trust God, our most challenging moments can build the character we need to bring others to Christ, knowing that His grace is sufficient to do what He has called us to do.

*Vision Beyond Measure*

# Daily Devotional

**Date:** _____

## Verse Reflection

## Application

## Prayer

## We are the Body of Christ

**Romans 12:5**

"So we, being many, are the body in Christ, and individually members of one another."

In Romans 12, Paul talks about the importance of operating, through faith, in the gifts that God has given each of us.

To operate in God's gifts, you must understand that, just as a physical body has moving parts, arms, legs, fingers, etc., that is also how the Body of Christ should operate. The Body of Christ comprises people who possess different gifts to make the body operate effectively. And each gift is needed to be a 'living sacrifice, acceptable unto God, which is our reasonable service."

If everyone truly understood how important their giftings are, they would understand that there is a place for them in the Kingdom and in the church—living peacefully among each other.

*Vision Beyond Measure*

# Daily Devotional

**Date:** _____

## Verse Reflection

_____
_____
_____
_____
_____
_____
_____

## Application

_____
_____
_____
_____
_____
_____
_____

## Prayer

_____
_____
_____
_____
_____
_____
_____

# God Can Still Use You

**Ephesians 2:10**
"For we are God's handiwork, created in Christ Jesus to do good works, which God prepared in advance for us to do."

Post my divorce, there were definitely moments of guilt and shame. I occasionally thought that God was upset with me because I was taught "God hates divorce." And as this is true, I failed to realize in the moment that God is and has always been the God of love and still loved me regardless of the decision I made after much thought, prayer, and counsel. After working through all of those feelings and emotions, and God healing my heart and brokenness, He revealed to me His purpose for my life, and I realized that He could still use me right there in the very place I was in and beyond.

Some people say they will live for God when they get themselves together, not realizing that if they could get themselves together without the help of God, they would have done it already. We are to repent where we are and move on, not staying stuck but learning from and turning from our sins and mistakes. God can still use you if you are willing and open to allowing Him to. The past cannot be undone, but with God's love and forgiveness, you can become a better person doing what

God has called you to do. In 1 Corinthians 7:23, the Bible says, "you were bought at a price; do not become slaves of men." And this includes being slaves to their personal opinions and thoughts of who they think you are and who you are not. God is still a God of promise, and there is no condemnation for those of us who are in Christ Jesus. (Romans 8:1)

# Daily Devotional

**Date:** _____

## Verse Reflection

## Application

## Prayer

## Flip the Switch

**Romans 8:11**
"And if the spirit of him who raised Jesus from the dead is living in you, he who raised Christ from the dead will also give life to your mortal bodies because of[a] his spirit who lives in you."

Many times we blame other people, blame our past, our parents, the devil, and sometimes even God as to why things are not the way we think they should be. When really, the outcome of our lives is due to decisions we have made. This comes to mind in Caroline Leaf's book, 'Switch on Your Brain' where she mentions, "we are not bound by the physical; we control the physical." (p 33). Additionally, she mentions how our thoughts control our brains, and our brains control our actions. Therefore, if we want something different in our lives and truly walk in the power that has already been provided to us, we have to think differently. Are you really thinking about what you are thinking about?

With that being said, we are given brand new mercies each and every day and new opportunities to walk in the power of God. If things are lining up with God's promises, we must become more aware of our thought processes. Are we allowing the enemy to sow the seed of doubt in our lives? Are we allowing ourselves to be subjected to fear? Are we listening to the voices of others who lack faith and allowing that to take root in our lives? God's grace and power are there for the taking. Let's flip the switch and walk in power!

*Vision Beyond Measure*

# Daily Devotional

**Date:** _____

## Verse Reflection

_____
_____
_____
_____
_____
_____
_____
_____

## Application

_____
_____
_____
_____
_____
_____
_____
_____

## Prayer

_____
_____
_____
_____
_____
_____
_____

## Keep Your Focus on God

**2 Corinthians 11:30**
"If I must boast, I will boast of the
things that show my weakness."

In 2 Corinthians, chapter 11, verses 16-29, Paul mentions the various challenges he endured while serving God. He highlights the abuse, hunger, and labor he experienced over time and even the persecution of those he thought were close to him. However, he finally says that he is not bragging about any of this but bragging about the power of God.

Many times believers tend to offer excuses as to why we cannot or why we do not serve God in our highest capacity. Some of us have been hurt by the church full of 'church folk' and use that as an excuse not to attend services or connect with other believers, naming the lack of trust as the issue. Then there are others who fail to see themselves as worthy to come before God just as they are, failing to truly understand the love of Christ. But Paul mentions that if he is going to boast about anything, it would certainly not be about the things he had gone through, but it would be about the power that worked in him during those times to make him more like God and to carry out the characteristics of His holiness. And this is how we have to live today. When things are not exactly the way we want them to be in our lives, instead of complaining, we should be encouraged to keep our eyes focused on what God is doing in our lives at that moment. Then thank Him for increasing our faith and growing in the power of His might.

# Daily Devotional

**Date:** _____

## Verse Reflection

## Application

## Prayer

## You are Free!

### John 8:36

"So if the Son sets you free, you will be free indeed."

In Galatians 5:1, Paul begins this section by reminding us to "It is for freedom that Christ has set us free. Stand firm, then, and do not let yourselves be burdened again by a yoke of slavery." (NIV) And here, I would like to call out the word 'again.' At the end of Chapter 4, Paul makes mention of the covenant of freedom that we, as believers, are born into. The covenant of being free and no longer bound by the chains of sin. Needless to say, we should never go back to living a life of bondage. However, there are those times when we have become free and begin to live a sanctified life, and people tend to place limits on our lives based on who we used to be. These are also the times when Paul tells us to stand firm in that freedom, not allowing anyone to hold you to your past.

I have seen and known people, personally, who have struggled to live for God because of the people around them who kept reminding them of the things they used to do. This caused them to feel a sense of guilt and shame and pushed them away from truly living in the abundant life God had for them. As leaders and believers, we must be careful not to remind people of their errors unless it is to teach a lesson they are open to learning or remind them of how far they have come. And at the same time, we have to be careful not to allow the enemy to remind us of our past to hold us back from living in abundance and the promises of God. I always say this: When the enemy tries to remind us of our past, remind him of his future. He is already defeated, and it is done!

*Vision Beyond Measure*

# Daily Devotional

**Date:** _____

## Verse Reflection

## Application

## Prayer

## Use Your Gift

**Ephesians 4:11-13**
"So Christ himself gave the apostles, the prophets, the evangelists, the pastors and teachers, to equip his people for works of service, so that the body of Christ may be built up until we all reach unity in the faith and in the knowledge of the Son of God and become mature, attaining to the whole measure of the fullness of Christ."

In the book of Ephesians, chapter 4, Paul provided instructions for those who have been called to preach the Gospel. He is encouraging each of us to carry out the calling and purpose that God has given us. It is important that we are purposeful and intentional in regard to how we operate, with authority, humility and discipline. But how exactly do we do that? How do we walk and operate in, fully, the purpose that God called us to?

First and foremost, we need to accept and truly understand the fact that we have a purpose. God has created each of us on purpose and for purpose. He said that He knows the plans He has for each of us, and that is to prosper us and give us hope. Once we have discovered and accepted our purpose, we must stay focused on the call. There are so many opportunities to compare ourselves to other people and feel that we should be so much further along than we are. We begin to compare our calling and level of calling to someone else's; we cannot see what God is doing in our own lives. Finally, we have to fight for our purpose constantly and allow the Holy Spirit to guide us on when and where we should operate and with whom. Sometimes, we will be tempted to use our purpose in a way that God didn't intend for it to be utilized, and that is when our purpose can be abnormally used or abused. And sometimes, the enemy will try to twist and contort the purpose we are called to. However, Paul goes on to say that each person should operate in the way that God has designed each of us, in our own giftings, being led by the Holy Spirit. When this happens, we are then "working within Christ's body, the church, until we're all moving rhythmically and easily with each other, efficient and graceful in response to God's Son, fully mature adults, fully developed within and without, fully alive like Christ." (v. 13, The Message)

## Daily Devotional

**Date:** _____

### Verse Reflection

### Application

### Prayer

## Give God the Glory

**Colossians 3:17**
"And whatever you do, whether in word or deed,
do it all in the name of the Lord Jesus, giving
thanks to God the Father through him."

There are times in our lives when we may have questioned whether or not a decision we were making at the time was right or wrong.  I have also questioned myself about what I was doing at a particular time, the God thing for me to do, even though it may have been a good thing. This scripture reminds us that sometimes we may not know the outcome of a certain decision, but when we do what we know to do, all in the Name of the Lord, the outcome will turn out just fine.  This reiterates the scripture that all things work together for the good. (Romans 8:28)

There are some who conduct themselves in the name of themselves, never giving God credit or acknowledging His strength and power. When we have the mindset to do everything in the name of the Lord, our decisions in life will be different. We will make better choices in which we truly live our lives.

*Lewana Harris*

# **Daily Devotional**

**Date:** _____

## **Verse Reflection**

## **Application**

## **Prayer**

## Be Bold in Your Faith

**1 Timothy 4:11-12**
"Command and teach these things. Don't let anyone look down on you because you are young, but set an example for the believers in speech, in conduct, in love, in faith and in purity."

In the book of 1 Timothy, there is a letter from his mentor and teacher, Paul, who provides Timothy with encouragement, instructions, and guidance regarding his ministry. Timothy was raised in a Godly household and had faith at a young age due to the imparted knowledge by his mother and grandmother. Because of his faithfulness and loyalty to the Gospel, Timothy became a great disciple of Paul and a trusted student.

However, specifically in Chapter 4, verses 12-16, Paul encourages Timothy not to get discouraged in his ministry simply because he is young. Paul reminds Timothy of the purpose and giftings given by God and to stay focused on what's most important, studying the word so others will see the growth and be inspired.

This particular portion of the scripture should be an encouragement to us because there may be times when you feel like an imposter, not fully confident in the gifts that have been given by God. I have felt this same way. However, over time, after truly accepting God's love and knowing God's perfect love casts out all fear, I have been able to walk in the authority of God, speaking and teaching boldly what God has wanted me to share with others. I have come to understand that my life is not my own, and I am here to do the works as stated in Isaiah 61: preach the Gospel, heal the brokenhearted, proclaim, comfort, and console. This is God's purpose for us.

*Vision Beyond Measure*

# Daily Devotional

**Date:** _____

## Verse Reflection

_____
_____
_____
_____
_____
_____
_____
_____

## Application

_____
_____
_____
_____
_____
_____
_____
_____

## Prayer

_____
_____
_____
_____
_____
_____
_____
_____

# Transformational Leadership

### Romans 12:6-8
"We have different gifts, according to the grace given to each of us. If your gift is prophesying, then prophesy in accordance with your[a] faith; if it is serving, then serve; if it is teaching, then teach; if it is to encourage, then give encouragement; if it is giving, then give generously; if it is to lead,[b] do it diligently; if it is to show mercy, do it cheerfully."

The Bible describes the spiritual gifts, specifically teachers, to equip God's people for the works of service. Additionally, in Romans chapter 12, the Bible also mentions that if one of your gifts is to lead, then you are to lead diligently. And Paul is a great example of teaching and leading Titus. In his letter to Titus, Paul exemplifies various leadership characteristics that we all could demonstrate as we minister to and lead others to Christ.

In doing research on Paul, it has been said that he was a transformational leader and change agent who always held great concern for others. In this particular letter to Titus, Paul shows his leadership skills by providing instructions on how to appoint other great leaders, delegate, be bold, and take a stand and guard against false prophets and rebels. And as Christian leaders, we could all take lessons from Paul on how to be inspiring, nourishing, and Godly, always promoting unity and love.

So many organizations promote individuals simply because of their technical skills, and then what is revealed later is the lack of people/human skills needed to lead their teams effectively. This lack of leadership effectiveness can cause organizations to progress and grow at a slower pace and create a high turnover. Therefore, what is needed in leadership development is not just the ability to get things or manage processes but the ability to lead and develop people to attain their highest potential and then teach them to do the same. Paul was a great communicator, which is probably the most critical leadership skill to have.

As we continue to grow within our own realms of ministry, life, and personal development, as mentioned above, we could all take lessons from Paul and become that transformational leader, one who inspires and motivates others to positive change.

*Lewana Harris*

# **Daily Devotional**

**Date:** _____

## **Verse Reflection**

_____
_____
_____
_____
_____
_____
_____
_____

## **Application**

_____
_____
_____
_____
_____
_____
_____
_____

## **Prayer**

_____
_____
_____
_____
_____
_____
_____

## You are Not Forgotten

### Hebrew 6:11,12
"We want each of you to show this same diligence to the very end, so that what you hope for may be fully realized. We do not want you to become lazy, but to imitate those who through faith and patience inherit what has been promised."

There have been times in my life when I have been tempted to quit my purpose due to circumstances that I experienced. I have lost, gained, and lost again. There were times when I questioned God's promises for me and even believed that I didn't deserve what was promised. Sometimes, I thought God had forgotten about me because I was comparing my life to others. But what I didn't know at the time was that I was sowing seeds of faith, even if it was the size of a mustard seed, because even though I wanted to quit ministry and the purpose I knew God had for me, I didn't. I tried, and it did not even feel right. I was more uncomfortable being out of purpose than I was in purpose, operating with little faith.

Over time, while staying connected to God, I continued to be diligent in my walk, sometimes even through my tears and began to experience God at another level. This raised my faith and provided more to my purpose.

I did not grow weary while doing good because I began to believe that in due season I would reap if I did not lose heart. (Galatians 6:9). And now that I know and BELIEVE God's promises for my life, I walk in a greater level of confidence that no one can take away.

*Vision Beyond Measure*

# Daily Devotional

**Date:** _____

## Verse Reflection

_____
_____
_____
_____
_____
_____
_____

## Application

_____
_____
_____
_____
_____
_____
_____

## Prayer

_____
_____
_____
_____
_____
_____

# Don't Get Weary

## Galatians 6:9
"Let us not become weary in doing good, for at the proper time we will reap a harvest if we do not give up."

One of the things that resonates with me in Paul's letters to Timothy is how he is always encouraging him not to lose heart in his ministry. Paul uplifts Timothy numerous times and is even vulnerable in sharing his own personal struggles. This level of relationship can be an example of great leadership where one chooses to follow another, not just because they have to, but because they choose to. This type of leadership created an environment where Timothy trusted and was loyal to Paul even until the end. And in 2 Timothy 3, Paul reminds him of this. He reminds Timothy of the evil and deception he will encounter while in ministry but still motivates and inspires him not to allow that to distract him from living on purpose and purpose.

This resonates with me because there have been leaders in my life that have encouraged me through trials, hurts, pains, and disrespect of ministry. I have experienced many things, but one that has stayed constant is the joy I have in encouraging those around me. I didn't and don't allow distractions to keep me from living the purpose God has for me because that is what He has called me to do.

Overall, we have to understand that "all scripture is inspired by God and is useful to teach us what is true and to make us realize what is wrong in our lives. It corrects us when we are wrong and teaches us to do what is right. God uses it to prepare and equip his people to do every good work." We stay in word, we stay focused, and we continue to do what God has called us to do to equip his people.

*Lewana Harris*

# Daily Devotional

**Date:** _____

## Verse Reflection

_____
_____
_____
_____
_____
_____
_____

## Application

_____
_____
_____
_____
_____
_____
_____

## Prayer

_____
_____
_____
_____
_____
_____
_____

# Now Faith

### Hebrews 11:1,2
"Now faith is the substance of things hoped
for and the evidence of things not seen.
For by it (faith), the elders obtained a good testimony."

In chapter 11, Paul is providing us with the definition of faith. However, we never mention verse 2 when it says that a good testimony is obtained.

Whenever I think of faith, I cannot help to think about the actions that are required to go along with it. You cannot experience or activate faith without action. Hence the verse, "faith without works is dead". (James 14:17, NKJV). When you activate your faith, you are walking in complete trust and confidence, knowing that whatever you are believing for, God will bring to pass based on His promises. This trust then becomes the evidence that other people see as a result of your faith. The evidence is the results that provide the good testimony mentioned in verse 2.

Paul then goes on to provide specific examples of individuals who operated in their God-given power and potential by activating their faith. Some of them experienced hardship, pain, and unbearable circumstances but still walked in faith. In The Message Bible, verse 3 says, "By faith, we see the world called into existence

by God's word, what we see created by what we don't see." As believers, we have to see God's promises in the supernatural before we can see them in the natural. We have to see it in the spiritual realm before we can see it in the physical realm. And we have to speak those things as though we already have them in possession, according to the promises of God. That is true FAITH.

*Vision Beyond Measure*

# Daily Devotional

**Date:** _____

## Verse Reflection

## Application

## Prayer

# Faith is Action

### James 2:14
"What does it profit, my brethren, if someone says he has faith but does not have works? Can faith save him?"

The word 'profit' simply means a valuable return or a gain. In essence, this scripture, to me, says 'what are you going to gain if you don't put actions with your faith". Many people who are 'in the church' say they have faith, but when it comes to walking it out, fear and lack of trust set in for various reasons. Maybe because no one in their family has stepped out of their comfort zone before. Or maybe they feel they lack the skills needed to be successful or whatever reason comes. But you have to walk in faith.

In the movie Indiana Jones, there is a scene where he is standing in a cave, trying to get to the other side. However, it appears there is no way to get across. Indiana Jones then makes the statement to himself, "it's a leap of faith," and takes a step. As soon as he takes a step, the entire bridge is revealed, and he is then able to walk across safely. This is a clear example of what faith looks like in the real world. God gives us a measure of faith, and we are to put action to it by taking that first step to gain a profit or a return. But what is the profit, or what is that return? It's all of God's promises. God's promises are there for us. Promises of abundant life, promises of peace, and healing. But we have to put action to it by speaking the Word, taking calculated risks, and sometimes doing those things to expand our comfort zone. If everything my hand touches shall prosper, I have to put my hand to something for it TO prosper.

## **Daily Devotional**

**Date:** _____

### **Verse Reflection**

_____
_____
_____
_____
_____
_____
_____
_____

### **Application**

_____
_____
_____
_____
_____
_____
_____
_____

### **Prayer**

_____
_____
_____
_____
_____
_____
_____

## Gifted To Serve

### Peter 4:10
"Each of you should use whatever gift you have received to serve others, as faithful stewards of God's grace in its various forms."

Everyone has been born with a gift or gifts to serve others in a way that will glorify God. In the Bible, it mentions that we are called to be a blessing to others, and when we fail to use our God-given gifts, we rob others of the things God wants to do through us for them. Just like people are drawn to the fruit of a tree, not the branches or the trunk, people are drawn to our gifts. And those gifts are our fruit that God has given us through the Holy Spirit. And just like the fruit of a tree, at its ripe stage, the gifts are able to provide encouragement to those in need.

So what can you do to use your gifts? First, find out what they are. What are you drawn to? What pulls on your heartstrings? What has God shown you? And sometimes, you can even take spiritual assessments to determine what gifts are stronger than others. Next, find opportunities to serve. Being in church all my life, all I know to do is serve. Through serving others is where you find purpose.

## The Gift of Discernment

### 1 John 4:1
"Dear friends, do not believe every spirit, but test the spirits to see whether they are from God, because many false prophets have gone out into the world."

The world, social media, the news, and a whole lot more, will try to get you to believe perspectives and ideas that go against the Word of God. And sometimes they sound REAL good. However, not every spiritual thought or idea is from God, and you have to have a spirit of discernment to determine what is God and what is not. This comes from spending time with Him, knowing His characteristics, and how He speaks to you personally. You have to determine what is false and what is true, and the only way to know this is to have a goal to operate in and by the Holy Spirit on a daily basis.

The Holy Spirit teaches us, guides us, directs us, reminds us of God's word in times of need, and gives us wisdom, revelations, and understanding. Not to mention a whole lot more, including guiding us to all truth. (John 16:13)

*Vision Beyond Measure*

# Daily Devotional

**Date:** _____

## Verse Reflection

_____
_____
_____
_____
_____
_____
_____

## Application

_____
_____
_____
_____
_____
_____
_____

## Prayer

_____
_____
_____
_____
_____
_____
_____

## You are Qualified

### 1 Peter 1:3
"His divine power has given us everything we need for a godly life through our knowledge of him who called us by his own glory and goodness."

In 2 Peter, Chapter 1, it is titled "Confirming One's Calling and Election." To be called or elected means to choose someone to hold an office or position by voting. And in verse 3, the writer mentions that God has given us everything we need to operate in the position we are called to. When we possess the qualities of goodness, knowledge, self-control, perseverance, godliness, mutual affection, and love, we have all we need to be effective and productive.

Many times, I have felt as though I was not qualified to do the things that God has called me to do. For example, a position at a job or past leadership positions. But one thing I have realized is that God will not just call those who are qualified, but He qualifies the one He calls. This passage explains that when we put all of these characteristics into practice, we become more productive in the Kingdom. Productivity creates results and fruit that people will be drawn to, and our fruit, along with God's word, will provide encouragement and nourishment for others.

*Vision Beyond Measure*

# **Daily Devotional**

**Date:** _____

## **Verse Reflection**

_____
_____
_____
_____
_____
_____
_____

## **Application**

_____
_____
_____
_____
_____
_____
_____
_____

## **Prayer**

_____
_____
_____
_____
_____
_____
_____

*Lewana Harris*

# Blurred Vision

### Philippians 3:12
"Not that I have already obtained all this, or have already arrived at my goal, but I press on to take hold of that for which Christ Jesus took hold of me."

Paul reminds us that our credentials, positions, titles, backgrounds, etc., do not matter when serving in the Kingdom. The important thing is being, what The Message calls, a "real believer", the "ones the Spirit of God leads to work away at this ministry, filling the air with Christ's praise as we do it." This resonated, personally, with me because I used to be the one who thought that if I was offered a higher title or role, I would be in a better position. My focus was to climb the corporate ladder and obtain a high leadership position until God revealed to me that I could lead right from where I was. The realization changed my perspective about my actions, and I became content, but not complacent, about where God had been me in that season. Things that were important to me were no longer a priority. Just as Paul mentioned in chapter 3, he didn't have it all together, but the goal was and should be to stay focused on learning and living Christ. Seeking the Kingdom first and knowing all things would be added. I love how Paul encourages us to keep "focused on that goal, those of us who want everything God has for us. If any of you have something else in mind, something less than total commitment, God will clear your blurred vision— you'll see it yet! Now that we're on the right track, let's stay on it."

I am at a place now where I want to see the fullness of God's glory in my life, my family's life, and everyone who is connected to me. I believe there is more, and I want to see God's hand in every part of my journey and be an example to my children and others of His goodness. I truly believe God wants us to live in abundance, and I don't want my life to be blurred because of my desire and wants.

# Daily Devotional

**Date:** _____

## Verse Reflection

_____
_____
_____
_____
_____
_____
_____

## Application

_____
_____
_____
_____
_____
_____
_____

## Prayer

_____
_____
_____
_____
_____
_____

## God is Still There

**Mark 8:20,21**

"'And when I broke the seven loaves for the four thousand, how many basketfuls of pieces did you pick up?' They answered, 'Seven.' He said to them, 'Do you still not understand?'"

In Mark 8:21, Jesus asked His disciples a very important question. He asked them, "Do you still not understand?" He asked the disciples this simple but profound question because even after they had just witnessed Jesus feed 4,000 people with a few fish and a few loaves of bread, they still questioned if the amount of bread, which was one loaf, was enough to feed everyone on the boat. Jesus had to remind them of what they had witnessed. Did they forget? They saw the miracle, but for some reason, they began to fuss and murmur about not having enough. And this is how it can sometimes be, as believers.

In my life, there have been challenging moments where I have gotten discouraged or unsure about a season in my life. However, I have learned that God has carried me through EVERY SINGLE TIME. So now, when the enemy tries to instill fear or unrest in my mind and spirit, I remember the character of God and how He has remained faithful in my life.

It's easy to focus on the natural things that occur in our lives, and the world wants us to always live in fear and uncertainty. But when you are saturated with the Word of God, under pressure, the Word is going to come out. And we then remember that if God has taken care of us before, He will do it again. As I have gotten older and more experienced, I understand that trusting God, praise, and worship is the best thing to do in those moments of uncertainty. I know He has my best interest in mind, and I know He will never let me down.

Additionally, another way to manifest God's promise of healing is to exercise your faith. This reminds me of the story of the woman with the issue of blood who was healed and made whole by her faith. "The act of faith is not only a physical act; it includes the exercise of the heart and mind toward God" (pg.135, Christ the Healer). This means knowing, speaking, and believing God's word even when we haven't seen the healing that we are praying for just yet. This means having a mustard seed level of faith to remove the issue hovering over our lives. Finally, as believers, by learning to be healed in these ways, we can "advance into a life of faith and usefulness in the Kingdom of God" and teach others to do the same.

*Vision Beyond Measure*

# Daily Devotional

**Date:** _____

## Verse Reflection

_____
_____
_____
_____
_____
_____
_____

## Application

_____
_____
_____
_____
_____
_____
_____

## Prayer

_____
_____
_____
_____
_____
_____
_____

# Be Silent and Trust God

## Luke 1:19

"The angel said to Zechariah, 'I am Gabriel. I stand in the presence of God, and I have been sent to speak to you and to tell you this good news. And now you will be silent and not able to speak until the day this happens, because you did not believe my words, which will come true at their appointed time.'"

I find this scripture profound because there are times when the Spirit of God gives me a revelation or speaks a specific word and the first thing I want to do is share it with others. However, in my spiritual growth and maturity, I have realized that there are some revelations that you are not to share until they manifest themselves and come to pass. This is because there are people who are believers but may not have the same level of faith that you have. Or it's just because God wants you to trust Him completely.

A great example of this happening to me was when I lived in Atlanta, going through my divorce and struggling financially. At that time, I knew I was supposed to move back home to Tulsa because that is what God was speaking to me at the time but I didn't want to. I didn't tell anyone that I was struggling until I was evicted from my apartment and forced to move back home where I had family support. This is the short version of the story but the point is, God told me to go back home and don't tell anyone about my financial situation but trust Me. And I did.

So many times sharing with other people what God reveals to us can cause frustration and confusion because of the 'other voices'. People don't mean any harm but they tend to insert their own ideas and thoughts onto us because they love us. Being cautious about what we share, to whom and when, increases our trust in God and allows us to hear His voice with more clarity.

# Daily Devotional

**Date:** _____

## Verse Reflection

_____
_____
_____
_____
_____
_____
_____

## Application

_____
_____
_____
_____
_____
_____
_____

## Prayer

_____
_____
_____
_____
_____
_____

## Take Dominion

**Genesis 1:28**
"God blessed them and said to them, 'Be fruitful and increase in number; fill the earth and subdue it. Rule over the fish in the sea and the birds in the sky and over every living creature that moves on the ground.'"

From the beginning of time and the creation of the earth, God called us to be fruitful and multiply and take dominion over everything on the earth. The definition of dominion means to have full control over something or to have supreme power or authority. Another way to describe this view is to see it as having jurisdiction to operate at a level of authority that is granted to you. This reminds me of when I was a probation and parole officer, having jurisdiction over the whole state of Oklahoma to arrest and detain those who violated their rules of conditions, as opposed to the local authorities who only had jurisdiction over the city and county they were assigned to. In my 'agreement' with the State of Oklahoma, I was ordered to serve, and in return, I was to operate in my level of authority. If I violated this agreement, my authority would be taken away.

I see this in our agreement with God when we became saved. We were given that same right and authority from the beginning and reminded again in Psalm 8:6

when the scripture says, " You (God) have made him to have dominion over the works of Your hands; You have put all things under his feet." Even though our authority is not officially taken from our hands, when we choose not to walk in this God-given right, we are living below our potential. Taking dominion over something such as our finances, our minds and thoughts, and everything in this earth, means we have to operate in the anointing and this takes faith. The anointing of God destroys the yoke of bondage and slavery the enemy tries to place upon us. Taking dominion means prospering in every area of our lives and excelling in places we never thought were possible and reaching our full potential. Taking dominion means that every relationship in our life is blessed and mutually beneficial. Taking dominion means that everyone who is sick is healed because of the power that we are allowing to operate in our lives and we EXPECT healing to take place. Taking dominion means we are living in the overflow and operating with no limits, because God has placed His hand upon us and has endowed us with powers given to no other creature.

*Vision Beyond Measure*

# Daily Devotional

**Date:** _____

## Verse Reflection

_____
_____
_____
_____
_____
_____
_____
_____

## Application

_____
_____
_____
_____
_____
_____
_____
_____

## Prayer

_____
_____
_____
_____
_____
_____
_____

## Renew Your Mind

### Romans 12:2
"Do not conform to the pattern of this world, but be transformed by the renewing of your mind. Then you will be able to test and approve what God's will is—his good, pleasing and perfect will."

Sometimes when a person makes a mistake or experience the consequences of a wrong decision, that person will lose faith in themselves and begin to live and operate from a place of defeat instead of the place of victory.

So how do we get back to that place when situations don't end the way we thought they would? We have to renew our minds. Merriam-Webster defines the word renew as 'to make like new, restore to freshness, vigor, or perfection'. We have to first take a step to restore our faith and intentionally remove ourselves from the old environments and old habits that have attached themselves to us. We also have to recognize and become aware of the current mindset that is no longer serving us.

Additionally, we have to rewire our thoughts by taking each one captive and saturate ourselves with the Word, apply it to our lives and change our behavior. This process will create those Godly habits that will bear and produce the good fruit we desire. This begins by reading, hearing and speaking the Word over each negative thought and situation in our lives. Through a closer connection with God, He begins to reveal truth and we begin to see ourselves as He sees us, not as the world perceives us.

## **Daily Devotional**

**Date:** _____

### **Verse Reflection**

_____
_____
_____
_____
_____
_____
_____

### **Application**

_____
_____
_____
_____
_____
_____
_____

### **Prayer**

_____
_____
_____
_____
_____
_____

## Be All Things

### Matthew 13:13
"This is why I speak to them in parables:
'Though seeing, they do not see...'"

In Matthew 13, Jesus' disciples ask Him he HE speaks in parable and stories instead of just 'telling it like it is.' And Jesus came back with a great reply in Matthew 13:11-13 saying, "Because the knowledge of the secrets of the Kingdom of heaven has been given to you, but not to them. Whoever has will be given more, and they will have an abundance. Whoever does not have, even what they have, will be taken from them. This is why I speak to them in parables: Though seeing, they do not see; though hearing, they do not hear or understand."

This is a great lesson for all of us when we are ministering to others. One of the things that I have is that we have to be all things to all people when we are sharing God and His goodness. To some who are mature in the faith, they will understand a little differently than those who are babes.

BibleStudyTools.com mentions a couple of reasons why Jesus taught in parables. "The first was to enable his followers to grasp the secrets of the Kingdom of heaven more easily. It was a teaching tool for them and us. And the presence of the Holy Spirit in the life of the believer continues to use these parables today to teach us the secrets of the Kingdom. His second reason was just the opposite. It hid the secrets of the Kingdom from those who had not committed themselves to his lordship. Parables allow those who have faith, along with the instruction of the Holy Spirit, to learn about the Kingdom. And they prevent others from doing the same. Those without faith and the Spirit are unable to understand the truths of Jesus' parables."

This was extremely profound to me as I continue to grow spiritually. It helps to keep in mind the level of spiritual and mental maturity of others when I am teaching or sharing the word, being aware of my audience, and sharing accordingly.

*Vision Beyond Measure*

# Daily Devotional

**Date:** _____

## Verse Reflection

_____
_____
_____
_____
_____
_____
_____

## Application

_____
_____
_____
_____
_____
_____
_____

## Prayer

_____
_____
_____
_____
_____
_____
_____

# Be The Example

## Mark 6:6

"He was amazed at their lack of faith."

There were so many thoughts and ideas that came from these chapters. However, one that stands out is Mark 6:1-6, where Jesus speaks about a prophet without honor in his own town. In these verses, Jesus is teaching, and as people were listening, they were so amazed at his level of wisdom that they began questioning His identity. Is that not just like church folks? Especially those who have known your past and try to bring it up every chance they get when they have seen you have transformed your life.

Fortunately, this does not happen in my family, but I have heard that the worst of these situations have been family members who tend to mention past issues. But one of the things that I have noticed is that the only reason why people bring up your past or begin to question the authenticity of your relationship with God is that it brings light to those areas where they are still lacking and need to improve on themselves, but for some reason, they just have not. This mindset causes jealousy and envy, which then leads to criticism and judgment. So what do we do with this? It says in verse 5 Jesus still walked in His purpose. He still laid hands on the sick and healed them but had pity on them because they lacked faith. And that is what we are to do. This brings to mind the scripture Acts 4:13, where 'they saw", "they perceived," but then "they realized."

I have learned that people are going to talk about you when you are doing something and even when you're not. But when you walk in the purpose God has for you, they will then know you have been in the presence of God, and you will be an example to them.

# Daily Devotional

**Date:** _____

## Verse Reflection

_____
_____
_____
_____
_____
_____
_____
_____

## Application

_____
_____
_____
_____
_____
_____
_____
_____

## Prayer

_____
_____
_____
_____
_____
_____
_____

## Heart Posture

### Luke 21:1-4

"And He looked up and saw the rich putting their gifts into the treasury, and He saw also a certain poor widow putting in two mites. So He said, 'Truly I say to you that this poor widow has put in more than all; for all these out of their abundance have put in offerings for God, but she out of her poverty put in all the livelihood that she had.'"

As Jesus continues to minister in parables, this particular parable shows just how much the position of the heart and how you give your time, treasure, and talents matters more so than what it is that you give. When Jesus speaks of this woman who is giving her last, it reveals that she is presenting an offering not out of fear but out of faith. And if more believers were truly honest, we have all been in that position where we had more months left than money and feared that if we gave our last, we would be unable to pay our bills. And these are valid concerns, especially when you are a divorced mother of three young children who is trying to figure out the next step.

However, as many times as I have been challenged financially, I have also seen the same amount of times, and more, of God's abundant blessings in our lives. I

experienced the move of God when I needed Him the most. And I believe that it was simply because of my faith and because of the Word that I believed when it said all of my needs would be met.

God looks at the heart and our motives behind what we do when we serve Him through our physical and financial gifts. And in this scripture, it shows clearly, that our heart posture matters the most.

*Vision Beyond Measure*

# Daily Devotional

**Date:** _____

## Verse Reflection

## Application

## Prayer

## JustOneWord

### Luke 7: 7, 8

"'That is why I did not even consider myself worthy to come to you. But say the word, and my servant will be healed. 8 For I myself am a man under authority, with soldiers under me. I tell this one, 'Go,' and he goes; and that one, 'Come,' and he comes. I say to my servant, 'Do this,' and he does it.'"

In this scriptural passage, the centurion's encounter with Jesus is one of true faith. He mentioned that his servant was sick, and He wanted Jesus to heal him. He believed that He was not at all worthy of Jesus even stepping into his home. However, the centurion knew the power of Jesus and believed that if Jesus said it, it would be done.

This is the type of faith that we need to be reminded of right now. So many of us, including myself, have sometimes gotten frustrated with how long things have taken in our lives. Whether it was a job promotion, new job, marriage, increased finances, or a new house, we have all been there. Failing to realize that when the Lord says it, it is done.

So how did the centurion even know this? Because he recognized the level of authority. He knew the impact of his physical authority as one who could lead soldiers under himself and give instructions, and they would do it. But he also recognized the spiritual authority that was much higher and more powerful, and all he needed to hear was 'one word.' Sometimes, that is all we need to hear is that one word from God because everything changes on that authority.

# Daily Devotional

**Date:** _____

## Verse Reflection

## Application

## Prayer

## You Can Be Restored

### John 21:17

"The third time he said to him, 'Simon son of John, do you love me?' Peter was hurt because Jesus asked him the third time, 'Do you love me?' He said, 'Lord, you know all things; you know that I love you.' Jesus said, 'Feed my sheep.'"

Jesus called out Judas and Peter as ones who would betray Him, even though both of them said that it would not happen. Though Judas went on to commit suicide, Peter is a great example of his personal conviction and the grace and mercy of God to restore.

Post his betrayal, Peter went on to become what some believe, the best of the twelve apostles, being the one who Jesus said, "Upon this rock, I will build my church." But why did Jesus choose Peter? I believe that, during his walk with Jesus, Peter experienced the characteristics of Jesus in a way no one else did. Peter was present during many or all of Jesus' miracles. Peter is the one who walked on water. Therefore, Peter knew the spirit of leadership required to spread the word of God. But for some reason, in one of his weak moments, he betrayed Jesus. And Jesus still chose him.

We have all been at that point where Peter was. We have all experienced Jesus' hand and presence in our lives in some form or another, but we have also had those moments where we tend to forget his power, and doubt or fear creeps in, causing us to make decisions that may not be the best. But I am so grateful for God's grace and mercy, which is new each and every day. The grace and mercy that still allows us to do what we are called to do, regardless of our circumstances, background, or any mistakes we have made; "And these signs will accompany those who believe: In my name, they will drive out demons; they will speak in new tongues; they will pick up snakes with their hands; and when they drink deadly poison, it will not hurt them at all; they will place their hands on sick people, and they will get well (Mark 16: 17,18)." This is our instruction.

*Vision Beyond Measure*

# Daily Devotional

**Date:** _____

## Verse Reflection

## Application

## Prayer

## Remove the Barrier

**Matthew 17:20-21**

"So Jesus said to them, 'Because of your unbelief; for assuredly, I say to you, if you have faith as a mustard seed, you will say to this mountain, 'Move from here to there,' and it will move; and nothing will be impossible for you. However, this kind does not go out except by prayer and fasting.'"

Right before Jesus said this, a father came to the disciples asking for help with his son who was experiencing seizures. However, the disciples were unable to heal the young boy due to what Jesus called a "lack of faith." Now, the disciples had been walking with Jesus and just observed Jesus heal the multitudes of people and feed the thousands, and still, Jesus called out their unbelief and lack of faith. But then Jesus encouraged them that, going forward, all they needed was a little faith to move whatever mountain came their way.

This Word is encouraging because it gives a key to success. This Key of Faith shows us that if we are bold enough to have the courage and faith to walk in what God has called us to do, we can get it done and accomplish it. So many times, we can get discouraged about completing a goal because we may not feel equipped enough. Or we don't start that business, take that new job, learn something new, or meet that new person because we sometimes choose fear over faith instead of faith over fear. God has given us everything we need to heal others, move mountains, live in abundance and wealth, and to succeed in everything we put our hands to. We have to speak what we know and remove the mental and physical barriers that keep us from moving and taking a step. God will be with us wherever we go, so it's a win/win situation.

*Lewana Harris*

# Daily Devotional

**Date:**

## Verse Reflection

## Application

## Prayer

## Speak The Word

### Luke 18:6-8

"The Lord said,'Hear what the unjust judge said, and shall God not avent His own elect who cry out day and night to Him, though He bears long with them? I tell you that He will avenge them speedily. Nevertheless, when the Son of Man comes, will He really find faith on the earth?'"

In Luke 18, there is the story of the woman who was persistent in going to the judge to get justice against her adversary. After her diligent pursuit of justice and her tenacity, the judge HAD to grant her the request she was seeking because he did not want to damage his character as a judge. The actions of what the Bible calls as the persistent widow, is what faith looks like. I am assuming that before she went to judge with her request, she already knew what she was entitled to. Therefore, she continued to ask and request based on the facts that she knew regarding the law. The Bible never said she pleaded, nor did it say she begged. She simply requested the judge to provide protection and justice. And after a while, the judge ended up granting her request because of her diligence. The widow's actions are an example of if we know the word and are diligently and fervently praying for what we understand about the promises of God in faith, He is faithful to provide the things we ask for simply because He is God. As believers, we have to operate like this persistent widow, constantly speaking God's word back to Him and believing that He will operate in the power He is to do exceedingly and abundantly above all we can ever ask or think. . Will the Lord really find that type of faith on earth? God is WAITING to bless His children and waiting on us to operate in faith. It's time to manifest on the earth that which has already been established in heaven.

*Vision Beyond Measure*

# Daily Devotional

**Date:** _____

## Verse Reflection

_____
_____
_____
_____
_____
_____
_____

## Application

_____
_____
_____
_____
_____
_____

## Prayer

_____
_____
_____
_____
_____
_____

# Forgive

### Matthew 6:15
"But if you do not forgive others their sins,
your Father will not forgive your sins."

"Just forgive and forget." That is a phrase that I, and many others, have heard over and over again since childhood. However, there are times, I believe, that forgetting is not supposed to actually happen. Why do I say that? Let me explain.

When we forgive others, it does nothing for the person we are forgiving but does everything for us. Forgiving someone means that even though someone failed you or failed to live up to your expectations, or hurt you, you are no longer holding on to the possibility of the situation having a different outcome. But forgiveness is a choice. A choice must be made over and over again until that situation no longer impacts us the way it did the first time it occurred. When I decided to divorce my ex-husband and move back home with my three children, I was urged by the Holy Spirit to forgive him and let go. I knew that I was moving into a new season and could not take the anger, bitterness or hurt into the chapter of my life. And because I forgave but did not forget, I have been able to inspire and encourage other women going through similar transitions in their lives.

God calls us to forgive and to cancel whatever debt we feel that person owes us. Additionally, the word says that if we don't forgive others, then God will not forgive us. (Matthew 6:15).

Forgiveness does not always mean reconciliation, but it does mean that whatever that person did or said to us is no longer holding us bound. We have to choose to forgive over and over, allowing God to cleanse our hearts. This is truly walking in genuine love.

# Daily Devotional

**Date:** _____

## Verse Reflection

_____
_____
_____
_____
_____
_____
_____

## Application

_____
_____
_____
_____
_____
_____
_____

## Prayer

_____
_____
_____
_____
_____
_____

CPSIA information can be obtained
at www.ICGtesting.com
Printed in the USA
BVHW050746280323
661281BV00002B/151